MacOS Catalina

Complete Manual to Operate Your Mac Like a Pro for Seniors and New Users

Tech Analyst

Copyright @2019

TABLE OF CONTENT

How to Use this Book

Welcome! Thank you for purchasing this book and trusting us to lead you right in operating the macOS Catalina on your Mac. This book has covered every details and tips you need to know about the macOS Catalina to get the best from your computer.

To better understand how the book is structured, I would advise you read from page to page after which you can then navigate to particular sections as well as make reference to a topic individually. This book has been written in the simplest form to ensure that every user understands and gets the best out of this book. The table of content is also well outlined to make it easy for you to reference topics as needed at the speed of light.

Thank you.

Introduction

With the introduction of the macOS Catalina, you now have more features to explore on your Mac like the **Picture in Picture** feature, New Dark Mode, Apple Arcade, option to unsubscribe directly in the Mail app and lots more. Even for existing users, these new features may seem a little overwhelming when using them for the first time.

In this user guide, you would find detailed steps on how to explore every available addition to the macOS Catalina along with pictures to make it easy for you to understand and follow. Whether you are just buying a new Mac device or downloading the new software to your existing device, this book has all you need to achieve more productivity on your Mac computer.

The MacOS Catalina was launched on October 7 2019 and available for users to download and install. Apple was kind enough to include list of devices that can download the MacOS Catalina. These devices include

- MacBook Pro
- MacBook Air
- Mac Pro from 2013

- iMac or Mac Mini from 2012
- 12-inch MacBook from 2015
- iMac Pro from 2017

Sidecar as a Second Screen

While the iOS is not merging with Mac, however, the new software has made it possible for both of them to collaborate. This feature is what the company called **Sidecar**. This feature has two sides. On the first side, your iPad can serve as a second screen for your Mac device using the Sidecar. As soon as both devices are paired, you can move a window to your iPad from your Mac which could be quite useful for reference purposes when working on a document. The Sidecar creates a sidebar on the iPad device that you can use to access the Control, Command and Shift keys. You can also use this to activate the Touch Bar on your iPad when needed. The second part of the Sidecar feature is that you can use your iPad as a markup and drawing device for your Mac. This simply means that you can mirror a document on your iPad from the Mac, then you can use the Apple Pencil to make drawings on this document and it would show on the Mac. Before now, the only way you could achieve this was to get something like the Wacom tablet but the new software has made this easier.

iTunes Split into TV, Music and Podcasts

For some time now, we heard the rumor that the iTunes would be overhauled and this happened with the MacOS Catalina after the Apple announcement in June 2019. The iTunes app has been divided into 3 individual apps: TV, Music and Podcasts. Apple's aim for doing this is to make it easier for developers to build apps that can work on both the iOS and the MacOS. Rather than have two separate sets of codes, developers now need to just tick one checkbox for their MacOS app to become an iOS one and vice versa. To sync your iPhone in the absence of the iTunes, simply connect your smartphone to your Mac and you would see all the syncing options displayed in the Finder Sidebar.

Auto Dark Mode

You can now automatically adjust the Dark and Light mode to suit the time of the day. The Dark Mode is a setting that applies on the whole system so it would reflect on the desktop as well as all your settings windows, Apple apps and any third-party app that has the feature enabled. This means you do not have to stress with clicking and manually changing the feature.

The Notes App

The notes app also has a new gallery view that displays the thumbnails for your notes to give you a quick view of every of your notes and their contents. If you need to work with other persons on a shared Notes collection, you can create a shared folder for this. Apple also confirmed that it is now easier and faster to use the search function of the notes app. Another feature is the new checklist feature that allows you to set some notes as completed. Once the notes are marked as completed, they are moved to the bottom of the list so that you can concentrate on the incomplete ones.

Improved Photos App

Some features were added to the Photos app like the new gallery view that arranges your pictures into tiles of different sizes while hiding the clutter in your library and presenting your best shots first. You can now browse your pictures by the month, day and year it was captured as the app makes use of machine learning to bring out your best shots within each period.

Reminders App

The reminders app was totally overhauled in the new software. It comes refreshed with new features that users would find helpful as well as a new design. The app now understands texts snippets like the time and date of a reminder and it can automatically create smart lists. Siri can also suggest reminders based on contents of the messages app.

Screen Time

Screen Time has been on the iOS and only just got to Mac with the MacOS Catalina. With this feature, you can limit the duration of time you can access the internet, apps and even the Mac itself. The aim of this feature is to help you place priority and focus on what needs to be done. When you launch the Screen Time, it would show you in details the amount of time you spend on your Mac for different apps. With that, you are able to know what takes your time on your device and what you should cut down on. You can go to the App limit section to specify how long you should be granted access to an app or feature.

Safari

The Safari browser has a new start page that shows both your favorites as well as frequently visited sites. This would make it faster for you to access your most liked sites. Siri suggestions would also come up on the home screen to include links and bookmarks from your reading list, links that came in via messages, iCloud tabs and lots more.

Find My

Apple recently combined the **Find My Friends and Find My iPhone** into a singular app they called the **Find My** in the iOS 13, iPadOS and MacOS Catalina. You can use this new feature to find both your friends and your devices. For all your friends that may have shared their location with you, you can navigate to the People section to see their location at the moment. With this new feature, you can find your device even if it is offline due to the encrypted, anonymous Bluetooth signal that the device sends out periodically.

New Accessibility Features

The MacOS Catalina also brings its own addition to the accessibility features. For one, Voice Control feature allows you to use your voice to operate your Mac. You can tell your Mac what you would like to do at a given time. There is also the ability to zoom text on a second monitor while maintaining the normal zoom level on the main screen. You can also hover on a text and click control to enlarge the text for easy reading.

Improvement on Security and Privacy

Apple is always concerned about safeguarding the privacy of its users and this was also maintained in the newest software. The MacOS Catalina has its own read only volume on the Mac drive that helps to keep the system files protected from being overwritten. Another thing is that apps would need your full permission to be able to access files in Desktop and Documents folders, external and iCloud Drives. Apple has further integrated the Apple watch with the Mac. For those that have an Apple watch, you can authorize stuffs like payments on your Mac by clicking twice on your Watch's side button. You can use this for opening locked notes, viewing passwords in Safari and approving app installations.

Chapter 1: Getting Started

How to Download and Install MacOS Catalina

- Ensure that your device is compatible with the new software. Follow the list of compatible devices in this book to confirm that your device is included.
- Ensure to back up your Mac before you begin the upgrade.
- Go to the App store on your Mac, search for MacOS Catalina.
- Click on the button to begin installation.
- When you see a pop-up window on your screen, click on **Continue** to start.
- The download would go straight to your application folder.
- As soon as the download is done, the installer would launch
- Then follow the instructions on your screen to install the new software to your Mac.

- You may need to input the administrator name and password when asked during installation so ensure you have it handy.

You can also download and install the new software from your system settings

- At the left upper side of your screen, click on the Apple icon.
- Select **System Preferences.**

- Click on **Software Updates**
- Then tap **Update Now**

How to Erase a Partition on Your Mac

Before you take any step, ensure to back up your system. Then restart your computer in the main partition to enable you erase the extra ones.

- Go to your dock and launch **Finder.**
- Click on **Applications.**

- Move down and click on the **Utilities** folder.
- Click twice to launch the **Disk Utility.**
- Choose the partition you want to clean out.
- Then click on **Erase.**
- Click on **Erase** again to confirm your decision.
- Then click on **Done.**

How to Create a Partition to Install MacOS Catalina

You can decide to run both the Mac Catalina and the Mojave on your Mac computer at the same time as Apple has made it easy with the built-in disk utility program. The steps below would show you how to partition your computer. To Partition your computer means splitting the hard drive into separate systems that are usable. It allows you to run two different operating systems on a single device like having the Mojave and the Catalina in one single device or the MacOS and Windows. Please note that when you partition your hard drive, you are also splitting the available hard drive space. So, I would not advise you to do this if you do not have sufficient hard drive space. Ensure that you have backed up your computer before you start and also confirm that you have enough free space for the second operating system, at least 30GB free for a start.

- Go to your dock and launch **Finder.**
- Click on **Applications.**
- Move down and click on the **Utilities** folder.
- Click twice to launch the **Disk Utility.**
- From the Disk Utility window, click on your hard drive usually named as "Macintosh HD" or "Fusion."
- Then click on the **Partition section.**
- You would be asked to either add a Partition or an APFS volume
- Select **Partition.**
- Then click on the (+) sign to Add Partition.
- Drag the resize control to modify the size of the partition you want to use, The blue color represents used space.
- Input name for the new partition.
- Confirm the file system format for the new partition. For MacOS Catalina, select APFS.
- Then click on **Apply**

- Allow some minutes for disk utility to effect the changes.

How to Remove a Partition on Your Mac

After you must have erased the partition, you can now remove it from your hard drive.

- Click on the main partition which is the first drive you would see on the list. Its often called "Macintosh HD" or "Fusion."
- Click on **Partition.**
- Choose the Partition to remove
- Tap the (-) button
- Then click on **Apply**
- This may take some minutes as Disk Utility checks the disks to make changes.

How to Switch Between Partitions

The steps below would show you how to move between the two partitions

- Click on the Apple icon at the left top side of your screen
- Then click on **System Preferences** from the available options on the list.

21

- Click on **Startup Disk**
- Tap the **Lock** icon at the left lower corner of your screen to unlock and make your changes.
- Input your admin password then click **OK**
- Choose your Partition Drive
- Then click on **Restart.**

How to Downgrade to the Previous Operating System

Step 1: Backup Your Mac

It is important to back up your computer before you delete macOS Catalina from your hard drive. Deleting the Catalina would erase any programs, files or documents that you did not back up on the Catalina. You can back up to an external drive or to cloud based programs like the iCloud, OneDrive or DropBox.

Step 2: Make a Bootable Drive for the macOS Mojave

First download the macOS Mojave from the Mac app store before deleting the macOS Catalina. Store the Mojave in an external hard drive.

Step 3: Delete macOS Catalina

Follow the steps below for this

- Connect your system to an active Wi-Fi or Ethernet

- Then tap the Apple icon at the left top side of your screen.
- Click on **Restart** from the available options.
- Press down the **Command+R** keys, continue to hold until your system reboots. Your computer will now enter Recovery Mode.
- From the OS X Utilities selector, tap **Disk Utility.**
- Select **Continue**
- Choose your **Startup Disk**
- Go to the window top and click on **Erase.**
- Input a name for the file you want to delete (macOS Catalina)
- Choose APFS from the list or **Mac OS Extended**
- Then click on **GUID Partition Map** if **Scheme** is available.
- Click on **Erase**
- Once done, click on **Quit Disk Utility** from the available menu in the left top side of your screen to return to the OS X Utilities selector.

Step 4: Reinstall macOS Mojave

- Connect your system to an active Wi-Fi or Ethernet

- Plug in the bootable hard drive where the macOS Mojave is stored into your computer.
- Then click on the Apple icon at the left top side of your screen.
- Choose **Restart** from the list.
- Press down on **Options** as the system restarts. This would take you to Options to choose a startup disk.
- From the list of startup disk, choose your bootable drive that has the macOS Mojave saved. This would start to install the macOS Mojave on your computer.
- Click on **Continue** in the installation window.
- Agree to the terms before the software can then reboot your system.

Step 5: Restore your backup

- Connect your system to an active Wi-Fi or Ethernet
- Then click on the Apple icon at the left top side of your screen.
- Choose **Restart** from the list.

- As soon as you hear the chime sound upon startup, press down the **Command+R** keys. Continue to hold until the system reboots.

- Click on **Restore from Time Machine Backup**

- Then click on **Continue.**

- Click on **Continue** again as soon as you have read the info about restoring backup.

- Choose the backup source where the backup is stored.

- Click on **Continue.**

- Click on the latest backup on the drive

- Then click on **Continue.**

- Your computer will start to restore the backup and then reboot.

How to Automatically Run Dark Mode

A new feature called the **Dark Mode** has been introduced with the MacOS Catalina to bring beautiful new color scheme to your Mac laptop. This feature has only two options: it is either On or it is Off. What this means is that you can turn on or off the Dark Mode automatically depending on the time of the day, such that, as soon as the sun goes down, the operating system in your Mac would turn to a classy dark theme to make it easy for your eyes to adjust. As soon as the sun is up, the light theme returns. Follow the simple steps below to enable this option:

- Go to **System Preferences**

- Click on **General.**
- At the top of your screen, you would see the section for **Appearance.**
- Click on **Auto** to automatically run Dark Mode.
- If you would prefer your Mac to be permanently on the Dark or Light theme, you can select your preference from this screen rather than selecting **Auto.**

How to Find a Lost Device with the 'Find My' App

The "Find My" app was introduced during the Worldwide Developer's Conference that held in July

2019. Apple confirmed how you can use this app to locate your lost Mac devices. This feature makes use of anonymized snippets of data transmitted from one Mac device to another until you are able to locate your missing device. The steps below would guide you on how to do this

- To launch the 'Find My' app, press **Cmd + Space** and then type '**Find My**' in the Spotlight
- At the left top corner of your screen, click on **Devices.**
- Then select the missing device.
- The missing device would be displayed on a map.
- Click on the '**i**' button on the map to display a list of options.
- Click on **Directions** to get to your missing device.

How to Unsubscribe from a Mailing List in Mail

As long as we have active email accounts, we are always tempted to sign up to several email lists. After sometime, we begin to receive emails that are no longer of interest to us but unfortunately, it is not very email sender that makes it easy for receivers to remove themselves from these mailing list. Thankfully, the

MacOS Catalina has equipped the Mail app with the ability to unsubscribe from these mailing lists.

Each time you receive an email from a mailing list, the Mail app would always include a bar at the top of the received email that reads "This message is from a mailing list," and would also include the "Unsubscribe" link. If you are no longer interested in that mailing list, simply click on the "Unsubscribe" link to unsubscribe from the list. This only works as long as the Mail app is able to identify every email coming from a mailing list.

How to Setup Sidecar to Use your iPad As a Second Screen

Another exciting feature of this new software is its further integration with the iPad. Sidecar allows you to pair an iPad to your Mac while it functions as a drawing tablet or a second screen. The steps below would show you how to set this easily.

- Ensure that your iPad is on the most recent version of the iPadOS.
- You also have to connect your iPad and Mac to the same iCloud account.

- After that, the icon would show up in your menu bar.
- Click on it and pairing would begin automatically, turning your iPad to a second Mac.

This settings for this feature can be found with the steps below

- Go to **System Preferences**
- Click on **Sidecar**
- From this screen, you can control features like shortcuts and touch bar controls

How to Sign Documents on Your Computer with your iPad or iPhone in Quick Look

- Click on the Finder icon to launch the Finder window on your computer.
- Locate the file you wish to sign and click once on it.
- Tap space bar on your computer's keyboard. You would see your document appear in **Quick Look.**
- Select the **Markup** button (a pencil-like icon).

- Then click on the **Signature** button.
- Select **iPhone or iPad**.
- Then click on **Select Device**.
- From the list of devices, choose your iPad or iPhone.
- Sign your signature on your iPad or iPhone.
- Then click on **Done** from your iPad or iPhone device.
- The signature would appear on your computer's signature menu. Select the signature.
- Pull the signature and drop it in its right place on document.
- Then click on **Done.**

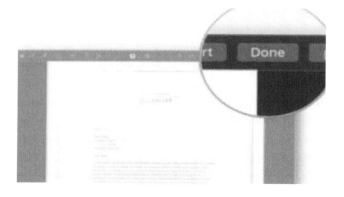

How to Sign Documents on Your Computer with your iPad or iPhone in Preview

- Go to **Preview** on your computer.
- Launch the document that needs the signature.
- Click on **View.**
- Then click on **Show Markup Toolbar** from the drop-down list.

- Click on the signature button.
- Select **iPhone or iPad.**
- Then click on **Select Device.**
- From the list of devices, choose your iPad or iPhone.
- Sign your signature on your iPad or iPhone device.

- Then click on **Done** from your iPad or iPhone.
- The signature would appear on your computer's signature menu. Select the signature.
- Pull the signature and drop it in its right place on document.
- Then click on **Save** to save the document**.**

How to Track Friends with Find My App

When you go to the People screen on the Find My app, you would see all the people that you have access to track.

- Go to the People's tab in the Find My app.
- On the left side of the screen, you have names of people you can track. Click on your preference.
- You have the option to view on 3 maps, satellite, hybrid and default.
- Use the plus (+) and minus (-) icon to modify the map size.
- Click on the location icon to display your current location.

- Tap the button for **Share My Location** to share your location with a new contact.
- Go to the To field and input the receiver name.
- For receivers not saved in your contacts, use the pop-up menu to add them.
- After adding the new receiver, then click on **Send.**

How to Track Your Device with Find My App

- Go to the **Devices** tab in the Find My app.
- On the left side of the screen, click on the device you want to track.
- You have the option to view on 3 maps, satellite, hybrid and default.
- Use the plus (+) and minus (-) icon to modify the map size.
- Click on the location icon to display your current location.

Chapter 2: How to Use Screen Time in macOS Catalina

While screen time has been available in iOS since 2018, it is only just getting to Mac. With Screen time, you are able to set up restrictions on how you use your device from setting up an app curfew on the devices belonging to your kids to blocking distracting notifications. The Screen Time is most used to block certain websites and apps that you use more often than is needed. This would give you the time to concentrate on other important things that needs to be done without the temptation of going to the blocked app or website, say for instance, Instagram. The steps below would show you how to enable this option.

How to Enable Screen Time on macOS

- Go to **System Preferences**
    - Then click on **Screen Time.**

- Navigate to the bottom left and click on **Options**

- Then click on **Turn On** located at the right top side of your screen to begin using screen time.

How to Disable Screen Time

- Go to **System Preferences**

  - Then click on **Screen Time.**

- Navigate to the bottom left and click on **Options**

- Then click on **Turn Off** located at the right top side of your screen to begin using screen time.

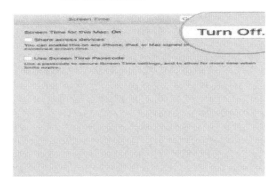

How to Add a Password to Screen Time

Adding a password to this feature would help to keep your settings safe and the password can also be used to extend screen time for other users when needed.

- Go to **System Preferences**
- Then click on **Screen Time.**
- Navigate to the bottom left and click on **Options**
- Check the box for **Use Screen Time Password** and set your preferred password.

How to Share Screen Time Across All Devices

To give you complete details on the total time you spend online, you can make use of the Screen Time feature on all your devices. When you do this, you can then see your total Screen Time from this app. Follow the steps below to enable this option

- Go to **System Preferences**

- Then click on **Screen Time.**

- Navigate to the bottom left and click on **Options.**

- Then click on **Share Across Devices**.

How to View Notifications Sent in Screen Time

If you want to know where your notifications are coming from, you can see that info from the Screen Time view.

- Go to **System Preferences**
- Then click on **Screen Time.**
- From the left side of the screen, click on **Notifications.**
- You would then see which apps sent notifications and the total number of received notifications by the day or week.

How to View App Usage in Screen Time

- Go to **System Preferences**
- Then click on **Screen Time.**
- Navigate to the left and click on **App Usage**

- On the next screen, you would see your app usage displayed by days, categories and apps. You would also find apps with limit on this screen.

How to View Mobile Device Pickups in Screen Time

If you have enabled the option to share the Screen Time across all your Apple devices, you can go to the Mac app to see the number of times you may have picked up your mobile devices with the steps below.

- Go to **System Preferences**
- Then click on **Screen Time.**
- At the left side of your screen, click on **Pickups**

How to Set Limits Using Screen Time

This setting allows you to choose the time limit for each app categories.

- Go to **System Preferences**
- Then click on **Screen Time.**
- At the left side of your screen, click on **App Limits.**
- Then click on **Turn On** to enable App Limits.
- Click on the **(+)** to add an app category.
- Then tick the box beside the app categories you want to place a limit
- After the app category has been highlighted, use the radio buttons to set your limits. You can choose either **Custom** or **Every Day.**
- Repeat the last two steps above for each category you want to place a limit.

- Then click on **Done** to confirm your selection.

How to Remove App Limits

- Go to **System Preferences**
- Then click on **Screen Time.**
- At the left side of your screen, click on **App Limits**
- For each category you want to lift the limit, untick the box beside it at the right.
- Click on **Turn Off** to disable app tracking.

How to Schedule Downtime Using Screen Time

Whenever Downtime is enabled, the only things that can work on your Mac are apps that you have given permission to work as well as phone calls. Follow the steps below to set up your downtime schedule

- Go to **System Preferences**
- Then click on **Screen Time.**
- From the left side of the screen, click on **Downtime.**

- Then click on **Turn On** to enable downtime
- Use the radio button to select either **Custom** or **Every Day** depending on your preferred schedule.
- If you select **Every Day,** it means that Downtime should happen at same time every day while the **Custom** option means that you can modify the time for different days of the week and even untick a box beside a particular day to disable **Downtime** for that day.

How to Set Always Allowed Contents in Screen Time

This setting allows you to make some certain processes available every time regardless of any existing restrictions. These processes may include communication with some apps or people. The steps below would show you how to set the **Always Allowed** feature

- Go to **System Preferences**
- Then click on **Screen Time.**

- At the left side of your screen, click on **Always Allowed.**

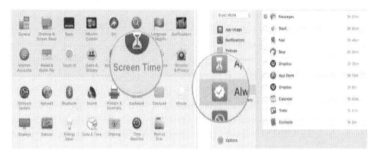

- Tick the box beside each of the desired items to **Always Allow**

How to Set Content and Privacy Using Screen Time

You can go through the Screen Time app to set your content and privacy with the steps below:

- Go to **System Preferences**
- Then click on **Screen Time.**

- At the left side of your screen, click on

  Contents and Privacy

- To enable the Content and privacy option,

  click on **Turn On.**

- You would find 4 options there: Apps,

  Stores, Content and Other. Tick each of the

  displayed boxes under each of the 4

  options,

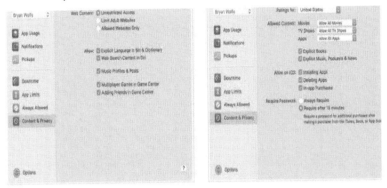

Chapter 3: How to Use the Music App

Apple splitted the iTunes into 3 different applications: Podcast, Music app and Apple TV apps. If you used the iTunes a lot, you may not experience difficulty in using the music app as the functions are alike.

How to Use Apple Music in the Music App

- Go to the applications folder or from your Dock to open the Music app.
- ➢ From the sidebar, click on **For You** to see the Apple suggestions and Mixes, playlists and albums recently played as well as what your friends are playing.

- ➢ From the sidebar, click on **Browse** to go through currently trending artists, other available music in the Apple library as well as Apple's playlist selections.

➢ From the sidebar, click on **Radio** to find and play Beats 1 radio shows whether previously recorded or currently live.

• From the Radio section, click on **Featured** to view featured radio stations, Apple's highlighted Beats 1 streams and radio contents recently played.

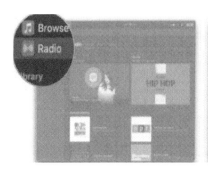 

• To access and play Beats 1 contents, go to the Radio section and click on **Beats 1**

• For available radio stations in the Apple music as well as selected partners, go to the Radio section and click on **Stations.**

- If you find any song you want to add to your library, use the + button beside the album, song or playlist.

How to Play Music in the Music App

- Go to the applications folder or from your Dock to open the Music app.
- Hover on a playlist or album to see the **Play** button. Tap the Play button.

- To play a particular song, click on the playlist or album.

- Then tap the **play** button.

How to Access Your Music Library in the Music App

- Go to the applications folder or from your Dock to open the Music app.
➢ From the sidebar, click on **Recently Added** to view songs and albums (minus playlists) added to your library.
- From same sidebar, click on **Artists** to look through the musical artists that owns music in your library.
- Select **View** from the menu bar.
- Hover your mouse over the **Sort Albums By** option.
- Select either **Genre, Rating, Title or Year.**
- Tap either **Descending** or **Ascending** and you are done

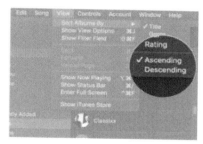

> To look through your music by the albums, go to the sidebar and click on **Albums.**

- Select **View** from the menu bar.

- Then click on **Show View Options**.
- From the drop-down list, you can choose to **Sort by:** Title, Year, Artist, Genre, or Rating.

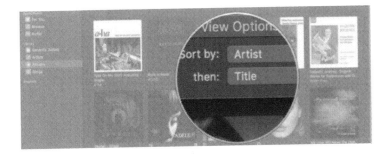

- Then go to **"Then"** and select from the options Title, Year, Artist, or Rating.

➤ To view all your songs, click on **Songs** from the sidebar.

- You can then choose to sort your sorts by choosing from the available categories: **Name, Artist, Time, Genre, Album**.

➤ From the sidebar, click on a **Playlist** to open it. You would see the available playlists sorted by their origin in the sidebar. Playlists created from iTunes would come first then the ones you created or subscribed to from the Apple Music would follow in alphabetical order.

How to Get Album and Song Info in the Music App

- Open the Music app from the Application folder or from your dock.

- Control or right-click on an album or song.

- Then click on **Get Info**

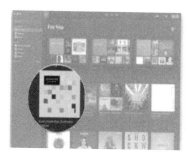 

- When editing more than one song, select **Edit Items**

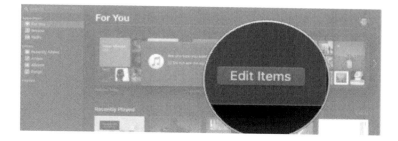

- You can choose to edit information saved under **Details, Lyrics, Artwork, Sorting, Options,** and **File** tabs

- Once done with the editing, click on **OK**

How to Import Music into the Music App

- Open the Music app from the Application folder or from your dock.
- Click on **File**
- Then click on **Import**

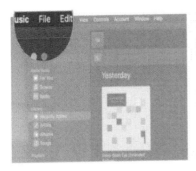 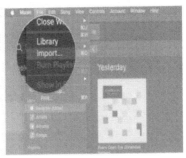

- Select the folder or file you wish to import.
- Then click on **Open**

How to Manage General Settings in the Music App

- Open the Music app from the Application folder or from your dock.
- Select **Music** from the menu bar

- Click on **Preferences.**

- Go to the **General** tab and tick the boxes to enable **Automatic Downloads,** turn on **iCloud Music Library,** and **Always check for available downloads.**

- Tick the boxes to hide or show Star Ratings, iTunes Store, Song list checkboxes.

- Click on the **drop-down** to choose the list size.

- Use the checkbox besides **Notification** to choose whether or not you want to be notified **when Songs Change.**

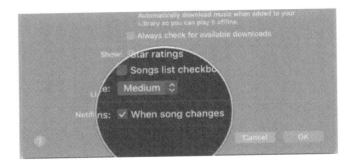

How to Manage Playback Settings in the Music App

- Open the Music app from the Application folder or from your dock.

- Select **Music** from the menu bar

- Click on **Preferences.**

- Then click on **Playback.**

- Tick the box beside **Crossfade Songs** to activate crossfading.

- Use the slider to go right or left to set how long you want the crossfade to last.

- Tick the box beside **Sound Enhancer.**

- Use the slider to go right or left and set the sound enhancement to high or low

- Tick the box beside **Sound Check** to activate Sound check.

- Use the drop-down menu on the next screen to select the quality of your videos when playing or the allowed quality when downloading videos.

- Tick the box beside **Use Listening History** to show your played music to your friends and followers as well as receive recommendations following the types of music you listen to on your computer.

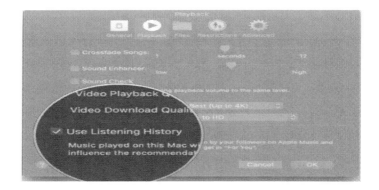

How to Set up Parental Controls in the Music App

- Open the Music app from the Application folder or from your dock.

- Select **Music** from the menu bar.

- Click on **Preferences.**

- Then click on **Restrictions**

- Tick or untick the boxes **beside iTunes Store, Music Profiles, Apple Music, and Shared Libraries** to enable or disable.

- Click the next drop-down button for **Ratings For** to pick your preferred country rating.

- Beside the boxes for **Restrict,** tick the box to restrict **"music with explicit content."**
- Then select your desired maximum content rating from the drop down.

How to Manage Music File Settings

- Open the Music app from the Application folder or from your dock.
- Select **Music** from the menu bar
- Click on **Preferences.**
- Then click on **Files**

- select **Change** if you would want to change the folder where media is stored.
- Use the pop-up window to choose a different folder for storing media in the music app.
- Then click on **Open.**
- Return to **Preferences** and tick the box beside **"Keep Music Media folder organized"** to have your music organized in the preferred library folder.

- Tick or untick the box beside "**Copy files to Music Media folder when adding to library**" to automatically add files that you drag into your library to the media folder.

- Then click on **Import Settings**.

- Click on the drop-down button to confirm the encoder format the imported files should come in: either **AAC, MP3, AIFF, Apple Lossless**, or **WAV**

- Then use the next drop down to set up the quality of the encoding.

How to Reset Warnings in Music App

- Open the Music app from the Application folder or from your dock.

- Select **Music** from the menu bar

- Click on **Preferences.**

- Then click on **Advanced.**

- Tick the boxes for **"Automatically update artwork" and "Add songs to Library when adding to playlists."**
- Then click on **Reset Warnings.**
- After which you click on **Reset Cache.**

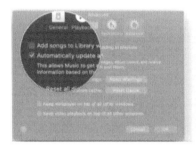

- Check the boxes for **"Keep video playback on top of all other windows" and "Keep miniplayer on top of all other windows."**

Chapter 4: How to Sync your iPad and iPhone with Your Mac

Even with the absence of iTunes, you can still sync your mobile devices with your Mac computer.

Where to Sync your iPad and iPhone on macOS Catalina

Rather than syncing your mobile device with the iTunes, you would now make use of Finder.

- From your Dock, click on the Finder app.
- Click on the name of your device at the left side of your screen.
- As soon as you click on this, you would see the interface that you are familiar with from the macOS Mojave.
- You can now manage backups, restore your device or sync content between the mobile device and your computer. You can also carry out file transfers from one device to the other on this screen.

How to Sync Movies Between your iPad or iPhone on macOS Catalina

- From your Dock, click on the Finder app.
- Click on the name of your device at the left side of your screen.
- Click on the **Movies** tab at the right side of your screen.
- To enable movie syncing, tick the box beside **Sync Movies onto your device**
- Under sync options, tick the box for **Automatically include**.
- From the pull-down menu, choose **All** to select every content or pick specific options from the list.
- Click on **Apply**
- Then click on **Sync** at the right bottom of the screen to sync your movies between your mobile device and the Mac

How to Sync Music to Your iPad or iPhone on macOS Catalina

Note: You cannot sync music on your Mac if using iCloud Music library sync on your iPad or iPhone.

- From your Dock, click on the Finder app.
- Click on the name of your device at the left side of your screen.
- Click on the Music tab at the right side of your screen.
- To enable music syncing, tick the box beside **Sync Music onto your device**
- Under sync options, you can choose either **"Selected playlists, artists, albums, and genres"** or **"Entire music library."**
- Go to **Options,** and tick the box beside **"automatically fill free space with songs"** and **"Include Videos"** only if you want.
- Then click on **playlists, albums, artists, and genre**, if applicable
- Click on **Apply**
- Then click on **Sync** at the right bottom of the screen to sync your music files between your mobile device and the Mac

How to Sync TV Shows to your iPad or iPhone on macOS Catalina

- From your Dock, click on the Finder app.
- Click on the name of your device at the left side of your screen.
- Click on the **TV shows** tab at the right side of your screen.
- To enable **TV shows** syncing, tick the box beside **Sync TV shows onto your device**
- Under sync options, tick the box for **Automatically include**.
- From the pull-down menu, choose **All Unwatched** to select every content or pick specific options from the list.
- From the next pull-down menu, choose either **selected shows** or **all shows**.
- If you clicked on **Selected Shows,** then tick the boxes beside the shows you wish to sync.
- Click on **Apply**

- Then click on **Sync** at the right bottom of the screen to sync your TV shows between your mobile device and the Mac.

How to Sync Audiobooks to your iPad or iPhone on macOS Catalina

- From your Dock, click on the Finder app.
- Click on the name of your device at the left side of your screen.
- Click on the **Audiobooks** tab at the right side of your screen.
- To enable **Audiobook** syncing, tick the box beside **Sync Audiobooks onto your device**.
- Under sync option, choose either **selected Audiobooks** or **all Audiobooks**.
- If you clicked on **Selected Audiobooks,** then tick the boxes beside the audiobooks you wish to sync.
- Click on **Apply**
- Then click on **Sync** at the right bottom of the screen to sync your audiobooks between your mobile device and the Mac

How to Sync Podcasts to your iPad or iPhone on macOS Catalina

- From your Dock, click on the Finder app.
- Click on the name of your device at the left side of your screen.
- Click on the **Podcasts** tab at the right side of your screen.
- To enable **Podcasts** syncing, tick the box beside **Sync Podcasts onto your device**.
- Then tick the box beside **Automatically copy**.
- From the pull-down menu, choose "**All unplayed"** to select every content or pick specific options from the list.
- From the next pull-down menu, choose either **selected shows** or **all podcasts**.
- If you clicked on **Selected podcasts,** then tick the boxes beside the podcasts you wish to sync.
- Click on **Apply**

- Then click on **Sync** at the right bottom of the screen to sync your podcasts between your mobile device and the Mac.

How to Sync Books to your iPad or iPhone on macOS Catalina

- From your Dock, click on the Finder app.
- Click on the name of your device at the left side of your screen.
- Click on the **Books** tab at the right side of your screen.
- To enable **Books** syncing, tick the box beside **Sync Books onto your device**.
- Under sync option, choose either **selected books** or **all books**.
- If you clicked on **Selected books,** then tick the boxes beside the books you wish to sync.
- Click on **Apply**
- Then click on **Sync** at the right bottom of the screen to sync your books between your mobile device and the Mac.

How to Sync Files to your iPad or iPhone on macOS Catalina

- From your Dock, click on the Finder app.
- Click on the name of your device at the left side of your screen.
- Click on the **Files** tab at the right side of your screen.
- To enable **Files** syncing, tick the box beside **Sync Files onto your device**.
- Under sync option, choose either **selected files** or **all files**.
- If you clicked on **Selected files,** then tick the boxes beside the files you wish to sync.
- Click on **Apply**
- Then click on **Sync** at the right bottom of the screen to sync your books between your mobile device and the Mac.

How to Sync Photos to your iPad or iPhone on macOS Catalina

Note: You would be unable to sync photos using your computer if you are using the iCloud Photo library sync on your iPad or iPhone.

- From your Dock, click on the Finder app.
- Click on the name of your device at the left side of your screen.
- Click on the **Photos** tab at the right side of your screen.
- Choose the files you wish to sync.
- Click on **Apply**
- Then click on **Sync** at the right bottom of the screen to sync your photos between your mobile device and the Mac.

How to Back-up your iPad or iPhone on macOS Catalina

Follow the steps below to manually backup your mobile device on your computer

- From your Dock, click on the Finder app.
- Click on the name of your device at the left side of your screen.
- Click on the **General** tab at the right side of your screen.
- Then click on **Back Up Now** beside the option for **Backup and Restore.**

How to Restore your iPad or iPhone on macOS Catalina

Follow the steps below to manually restore your mobile device on your computer

- From your Dock, click on the Finder app.
- Click on the name of your device at the left side of your screen.
- Click on the **General** tab at the right side of your screen.
- Then click on **Restore Back Up** beside the option for Backup and Restore.

Chapter 5: How to Use the Podcasts App on Mac

The Podcast app is another segment that was broken out of the iTunes. The app allows you to search for, subscribe to and manage your podcast library. The app interface is similar to that of the iOS podcast app. The steps below have been broken down to guide you on everything regarding podcasts on your computer.

How to Play a Podcast in the Podcast App

It is quite easy to play a podcast whether downloaded or not.

- You can open the podcasts app from the launchpad, Dock or application folder.
- Then click on the podcast photo of your desired podcast.
- Regardless of the tab you are in at the time, whether searching for a new podcast or looking for your last podcast, whenever you click on a podcast, the app would automatically begin to play the podcast.

How to Search for Podcast from your Podcast Library

Follow the steps below to find an episode of a podcast available in your library.

- Open the podcasts app from the launchpad, Dock or application folder.
- From the sidebar, click on the search bar.

- Then click on **Your Library.**
- Input your search keyword.
- Then click **Enter** on your keyboard.

How to Search for a Podcast from the App

You can use the search bar to find a new podcast.

- Open the podcasts app from the launchpad, Dock or application folder.
- From the sidebar, click on the search bar.

- Input your search keywords.
- Then click **Enter** on your keyboard.
- The next screen would show all the available options for the episodes and shows related to the search keyword.

How to Subscribe to a Podcast

When you subscribe to a podcast, the podcast would automatically be added to your library. This means that you would always see new episodes and be able to listen to them as they are released.

- Open the podcasts app from the launchpad, Dock or application folder.
- Search for the podcast you desire to subscribe to.

- Hover your mouse over the **Podcast photo** until you see the **Play and Option** button.
- Then click on **Options** (this is the 3 dots on your screen as shows in the screenshot below)
- Click on **Subscribe.**

How to Unsubscribe to a Podcast

You can choose to unsubscribe from a podcast whenever you want. It would not remove the podcast from your library but new episodes would not be automatically added to your library.

- Open the podcasts app from the launchpad, Dock or application folder.
- Search for the podcast you desire to unsubscribe in your library

- Hover your mouse over the **Podcast photo** until you see the **Play and Option** button.
- Then click on **Options** (this is the 3 dots on your screen as shows in the screenshot below)

- Click on **Unsubscribe.**

How to Play a Podcast Next in Queue from the App

- Open the podcasts app from the launchpad, Dock or application folder.

- Search for the podcast episode you desire to play next in your library
- Hover your mouse over the **Podcast photo** until you see the **Play and Option** button.
- Then click on **Options** (this is the 3 dots on your screen as shows in the screenshot below)
- Click on **Play Next**.

How to Delete a Podcast from Your Podcast Library

- Open the podcasts app from the launchpad, Dock or application folder.
- Search for the podcast you desire to delete in your library

- Hover your mouse over the **Podcast photo** until you see the **Play and Option** button.

- Then click on **Options** (this is the 3 dots on your screen as shows in the screenshot below)

- Click on **Delete from library.**

How to Share a Podcast in the App

Follow these steps to share podcast to your friend via email, messages, Notes, AirDrop or any other preferred method.

- Open the podcasts app from the launchpad, Dock or application folder.

- Look for the podcast you wish to share.

- Hover your mouse over the **Podcast photo** until you see the **Play and Option** button.

- Then click on **Options** (this is the 3 dots on your screen as shows in the screenshot below)
- Click on **"Share Show"** or **"Share Episode."**

- Select your preferred sharing method.
- Depending on the selected method, you may need to type in some more info. This is different for each method.

How to View Top Charts in the Podcasts App

From your podcast app, you can update yourself with what is trending and hot in the podcast world.

- Open the podcasts app from the launchpad, Dock or application folder.
- From the sidebar, click on **Top Charts**.

- The screen would display the top shows and episodes of podcasts that other Podcasts users are listening to.

How to Change the Play Order of Episodes in the Podcasts App

- Open the podcasts app from the launchpad, Dock or application folder.
- Go to your library and look for the podcast you do not want to receive notifications from.
- Hover your mouse over the **Podcast photo** until you see the **Play and Option** button.

- Then click on **Options** (this is the 3 dots on your screen as shows in the screenshot below)
- Click on **Settings**.
  - Select your desired options for the episodes. you can choose from any of the 4 options below: **Play Most Recent First, Play in Sequential Order, Custom Settings** or **Only Keep the Most Recent Episodes.**

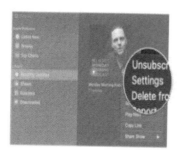 

Chapter 6: How to Use the Apple TV App for Mac

The Apple TV which has been available on iOS is now available on Mac too. You can watch your favorite channel titles or library right from your computer. Your progress on movies and shows would sync across your iPad, iPhone, Mac and the Apple TV so that you can always resume from the last watched content regardless of the device you are viewing from. There is however one main difference between the TV app on your Mac and that of the other devices. The TV app on the Apple TV, iPad and iPhone integrates with several third-party apps like NBC and Hulu to give you multiple options in one single app. This feature however is not available with the TV app for your computer.

How to Play a Video from Your Library in the TV App

Thankfully, you no longer have to go to the separate TV shows and Movies app to watch contents you purchased on the Apple TV.

- From the TV app, click on **Library** located at the top side of your screen.

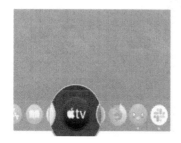 

- You would see the following options in the sidebar:

➢ TV Shows: a collection of all your purchased TV shows

➢ Movies: a collection of all your purchased movies

➢ Recently Added: TV shows and Movies that were recently added to your personal content library.

➢ Genres: choose from the available genres. Each genre has both TV shows and movies that belongs to the chosen genre.

➢ Downloaded: TV shows and movies you downloaded to your computer to view when offline.

- Click on the show or movie you desire to watch.

- Hover your mouse on the chosen episode or movie until you see the play button. Click on the play button and the show or TV would download and begin to play.

How to Watch a Movie or Show in the TV App

Follow the simple steps below to get started.

- Launch the TV app from the applications folder or from your Dock.

- Click on a movie or TV show from the **Up Next** section to start watching it instantly.

- You can also navigate to **What to Watch** or any other section for movie and TV.

- Click on your preferred movie or show.
- Then click the **Play** button.

How to Add Movies and Shows to Up Next

When searching for what to watch, your first stop should be **Up Next.** It gives you the latest episodes of your most loved shows or helps you resume the last movie you were watching.

- Launch the TV app from the applications folder or from your Dock.
- Play a TV show or movie from the app to add the movie to the **Up Next** section.
- Otherwise, you can click on a movie or content in any of the sections under **Up Next**
- Then click on **Add to Up Next.**

How to Buy TV Shows and Movies in the TV app

Apart from watching contents that you have bought in the past, you can also buy TV shows and movies in your app.

- From the TV app, click on **TV Shows** or **Movies** at the top of your screen.
- Select the title you wish to rent or buy.
- Click on **Rent** or **Buy** once its available.
- Alternatively, use the search bar and type the name of your desired title.
- Select the title from the search results.
- Click on **Rent** or **Buy** once its available.

How to Subscribe to a Channel in the TV App

Similar to what you have on the Apple TV, iPad or iPhone, You can also subscribe to channels like the Cinemax, EPIX and Showtime.

- Go to the TV app.
- Under **Apple TV Channels,** click on the channel you wish to subscribe to.
- Then select **Try It Free**.
- Input your password.
- Then click on **Buy.**

- Click on **Confirm** to accept.
- After the free trial period, you would begin to get charged for subscription. You would also receive content recommendations

from the channel in the **Watch Now** part of the TV app.

How to Cancel a Channel Subscription on Your Mac

To cancel free trail or unsubscribe from a channel, follow the steps below

- Go to **System Preferences** from the application folder or Dock
- Click on **Apple ID.**
- Select **Media & Purchases.**
- Beside **Subscriptions,** click on **Manage.**
- beside **channel subscription**, Tap **Edit** on your list of active subscriptions. When cancelling during a free trial, you would find this at the end of the list.
- Click on **Cancel Subscription**.
- Then click on **Confirm** to accept.

How to Manage Video Playback Settings in the TV App

- From the Apple TV app, click on TV in the menu bar.

- Click on **Preferences.**

- Then select **Playback.**

- Beside **Streaming Quality,** click on the drop-down to set the streaming media quality to either Good or Best Available.

- Beside **Download Quality,** click on the drop-down to set the streaming media quality to either **Up to SD, Up to HD, Up to SD,** or **Most Compatible Format.**

- Tick the boxes to set if the TV apps should download HDR content and multichannel audio.

- Tick the boxes if you want the TV app to be able to use your view history to set recommendations.

How to Manage Downloads in the TV Apps

- From the TV app, click on **TV** in the menu bar.

- Select **Preferences**.

- If you want the app to always look for available downloads, go to the **General** section and then tick the box beside **Always check for available downloads.**

- You can choose to select both or either the **TV Shows** and **Movies** boxes to automatically download both or automatically download only TV episodes or movies.
- Tick the box beside "Checkboxes in Library" to automatically sync only items in your library that you have checked.
- Tap the drop-down button to select a new list size.

How to Manage Media Files in the TV App

- From the Apple TV app, click on TV in the menu bar.
- Click on **Preferences.**
- Then select **Files**.
- To change the folder where media contents are stored in the TV app, click on **Change** or click on **Reset** to return the folder to its default location.

- If changing folder, choose a different folder for media storage from the pop-up window.

- Then click on **Open.**

- Return to **Preferences,** tick or untick the box beside **Keep Media folder organized** to have your media organized in the new library folder.

- Tick or untick the box beside "**Copy files to Media folder when adding to library"** to automatically add files that your drag into your library to the media folder.

- Tick the last box if you want the TV shows and movie files to be automatically deleted once you are done watching them.

How to Reset Warnings, Clear Cache and Play History in TV App

- Open the TV app from the Application folder or from your dock.
- Select **TV** from the menu bar
- Click on **Preferences.**
- Then click on **Advanced.**

- Then click on **Reset Warnings**.
- After which you click on **Reset Cache**.
- And click on **Clear Play History**.

How to Set up Parental Controls in the TV App

- From the Apple TV app, click on TV in the menu bar.
- Click on **Preferences.**
- Then click on **Restrictions.**

- Tick or untick the boxes beside **Shared Libraries** and **Purchasing or Subscription** to enable or disable.

- Click the next drop-down button for **Ratings For** to pick your preferred country rating.

- Beside the boxes for **Restrict,** tick the box to restrict TV shows and movies to defined ratings.

- Then use the drop down to choose the maturity limits of ratings for TV shows and movies.

Chapter 7: How to Use Notes App on Mac

The Notes app allows you to save information quickly from shopping list to thoughts and ideas. You can also secure your notes, lock the ones with password to be viewed by only you. You can also sync your notes across all your Apple devices. The guides below would show you how to maximize the Notes app on your computer.

How to Start a New Note

- Open the Note app from the Application folder or from your dock.
- Then click on the button for **New Note** (a pencil icon in a square)
- You can also click on **File** from the menu bar at your screen top and then click on **New Note**.
- Begin writing on your note.

How to Make a Checklist

- Open the Note app from the Application folder or from your dock.

- Then click on the button for **New Note** (a pencil icon in a square)
- You can also click on **File** from the menu bar at your screen top and then click on **New Note**.
- Click on the checklist button (a checkmark icon in a circle)
- Then type in your first item.
- Tap **Enter** on your keyboard to start a new checklist item automatically.

How to Reorder Checklist Notes

- Launch the checklist you wish to re-order from the notes app.
- Then click and hold down on the box beside the checklist item you desire to move.
- Pull the checklist item to your preferred position. Do this until you have arranged the list to your satisfaction.

How to Make a Dashed, Bulleted or Numbered Headings and List

- Open the Note app from the Application folder or from your dock.
- Then click on the button for **New Note** (a pencil icon in a square)
- You can also click on **File** from the menu bar at your screen top and then click on **New Note**.
- In the menu bar, click on **Format.**
- Select **Heading** from the drop-down list to convert the next line in the note into a heading.
- Tick either **Numbered List, Dashed List** or **Bulleted List** for your preferred list type.
- To stop writing in a list, tap the **Return** button on your keyboard while on a blank list item.

How to Create Password for Locked Notes

- Open the Note app from the Application folder or from your dock.

- Click on **Notes** from the menu bar and then click on **Preferences**.
- Click on **Set Password**.
- Then type in your new password.
- Type in the password again in the field for **Verify**.
- You can choose to set up a password hint.
- Then click on **Set Password**.

How to View Note Attachments

- Open the Note app from the Application folder or from your dock.
- In the toolbar, you would find the Attachment button, looks like 4-square, click on it.

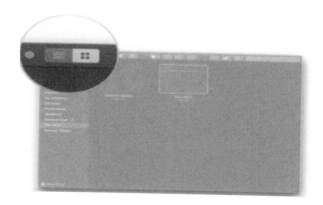

- Click on any of the different tabs like **Sketches, Photos & Videos**, and **Audio** to see your attachments.

How to Lock a Note

- From the Notes app, select the Note you want to lock.
- Navigate to the toolbar and click on the Lock icon, like a padlock image, to lock your Note.

How to Sign in to iCloud

- Open the **System Preferences** either from the Dock or go to the menu button at the left top side of your screen and then click on **System Preferences**.
- Select **iCloud**.

- Input your login credentials to sign in.
- Ensure to tick the box beside **Notes** under the iCloud menu after signing in.
- You can also sign into iCloud on your iPad and iPhones to sync your notes across all your devices.

How to Invite Others to Collaborate on a Note

MacOS Catalina allows you to not only invite people to collaborate but to also collaborate on a complete folder in the Notes app. Before you can collaborate on the note app, other invitees must be using iPhone, Mac or iPad.

- From the Notes app, open the Note you would like to add people to.

- In the toolbar, click on the button to Add people (a silhouette icon with a "+" beside it).

- Select either **Folder "[folder name]** or **Note "[note name]** to share that folder or note.
- Select the method to share the invite (a link, message, mail and so on)
- From the permission drop down menu, chose what the invited persons can do with the note, whether they can make changes or just read.
- Then click on **Share.**
- Input the phone number or email address of the persons you want to share the note with.
- Click on **Send.**

How to Send Note to Another App or Person

- Go to the notes app and select the notes for sharing.
- Tap the share button from the toolbar (this looks like a square with a shooting out arrow)
- Select the app to use for sharing the note.

How to View Notes in a Gallery

With the macOS Catalina, you have a gallery view that allows you view your notes in a fashion that is more visually dynamic.

- First open the notes app.
- Then launch the folder you would like to have the gallery view.
- At the left top side of the toolbar, click on the gallery button.
- You can return the folder to the list view by clicking on the List button.

How to Sync Notes to iCloud in macOS Catalina

- Go to System Preferences.
- Then click on **Apple Account**.

- Login to your **iCloud account** if not logged in already.

- Then click on iCloud.

- Tick the box besides Notes if unchecked.

Chapter 8: How to Use Reminders App on Mac

In this part of the book, you would learn important aspects of the Reminders app on your computer. The reminders app can be used to make your shopping lists, track most important tasks and several other functions. The iCloud and other services can be used to sync your to-do list across your iPad, iPhone and Mac devices.

How to Create a Reminder

- Go to your Dock and launch Reminders.
- Then click the Plus "+" button.

- Type your reminder and save

How to Add Reminders Account Provider

- Go to your Dock and launch Reminders

- Click on **Reminders** from the menu bar.

- Then click on **Add Account.**
- Select the Reminders account type you want, for example, iCloud.
- Then click on **Continue.**
- Input your login credentials then sign in.

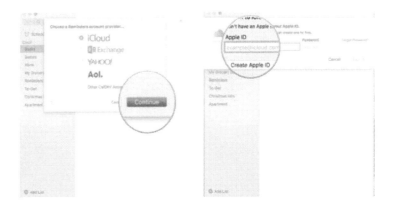

- Check that the box beside Reminders is ticked already, if not, tick the box and choose the app you want your account to be used with.

- Then click on **Add Account.**

How to Set up Location Notification for a Reminder

- Go to your Dock and launch Reminders.
- Select the text for the reminder you want to add the location.
- Then click on **Add Location.**
- You can either choose from the suggestions if it suits your need or just type your own location manually.
- Then click on the suggestion that comes up on the list.

How to Schedule Due Date for a Reminder

- Go to your Dock and launch Reminders.
- Select the text for the reminder you want to add the date.
- Then click on **Add Date.**
- You can either choose from the suggestions or just type your own date.
- Then click on **Add Time.**
- Choose from the suggestions or just type your own time.

How to Create a New List

- Go to your Dock and launch Reminders.
- Then click on **Add List**.
- Type your preferred name for the list.

How to Rename a List

- Go to your Dock and launch Reminders.
- Right click with your mouse on the list you desire to rename.
- Then click on **Rename** and input the new name.

How to Delete a List

- Go to your Dock and launch Reminders.
- Right click with your mouse on the list you desire to delete.
- Then click on **Delete**.

How to Share a List with Another iCloud User

- Go to your Dock and launch Reminders.
- click with your mouse on the **Share** button beside the list you want to share. The share button would come up when you hover your cursor on the name of the existing list.
- Select the method you would like to share the list with, either Airdrop, Copy Link, Messages or Mail.

- For Messages or Mails, click on **Share.**
- Input the name, phone number or email address of the receiver.
- Then click on **Send.**
- If using **AirDrop** or **Copy Link**, Input the name, phone number or email address of the receiver.

- Then click on **Share.**

How to Move a Reminder to another List

- Go to your Dock and launch Reminders.
- click with your mouse on the list that has the reminder you want to move.
- Click and hold down on the reminder you want to move.
- Pull the reminder over the new list you want it at.

How to Use Text Snippets in Reminder

Before the launch of this current software, the Reminders app was nothing exciting. It was just the ordinary reminders app without any extra feature. Now, the Reminders app has been completely redesigned to add some handy new features that were not there before. One of such features is being able to understand text snippets. Rather than typing your reminder, then manually set the location, time and other features, you can now type these details in natural language and they would be added automatically. For instance, you can type, "Date with Michelle tomorrow at McDonald's for 5pm," the reminders app will now create a reminder and also give you suggestions to set the time and date to tomorrow for 5pm. This is pretty cool and simple.

How to Group Reminder Lists

- From the Reminders app, click and pull one list on another list.
- Then input a name for the new group.

How to Add a Message Notification for Reminders

This is similar to the iOS 13. You can choose to be reminders the next time you message a specified contact.

- Hover your cursor on the reminder you wish to add to the message notification, then click on the "**i**" button that appears.

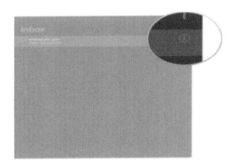

- Check the box beside **When Messaging a Person**
- Select the name of the contact.
- Type the contact's name or scroll through the list.
- Click on the desired contact.

How to Add Attachments to Reminder

- Hover your cursor on the reminder you wish to add to the message notification, then click on the "**i**" button that appears.

- Click on **Add Image**.

- Select **Photos** to go through your Photo library and add photos.
- Click either **Add Sketch, Scan Documents,** or **Take Photo** under the iOS devices to create images directly on the iOS device

and import these images from the iOS
device.

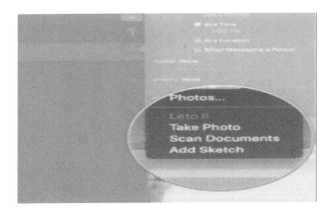

**How to Add a Secondary Reminder to an Existing
one**

Follow the steps below to create a sub-reminder
under an existing one.

- Go to your Dock and launch Reminders.
- In the same list as the existing reminder,
  create another reminder.
- Click and hold down on the new reminder.
- Pull the new reminder to the existing
  reminder.
- Use the chevrons to hide or show the sub
  reminder

Chapter 9: How to Use Voice Controls on Mac

MacOS Catalina allows you to control your computer with your voice with the use of speech commands. This new feature is would be beneficial to persons that has limited mobility, dexterity and other conditions. It is also another great way you can interact with your computer.

How to Turn on Voice Control

You have to first set up this feature to be able to enjoy the benefits. Follow the steps below:

- From the system Dock, click on **System Preferences**
- Tap on **Accessibility**.
- Under the section for Motor, click on **Voice Control** at the left side.
  - Then tick the box beside **Enable Voice Control** to activate this feature.

How to Change the Voice Control Language on Mac

This feature uses your computer's language as its default language when setting up. Follow the steps below to change this:

- From your system Dock, click on **System Preferences**
- Click on **Accessibility**.
- Under the section for Motor, click on **Voice Control** at the left side.
- Use the drop-down option beside Language.
- Click on **Customize.**
- Select the languages you wish to add.
- Then click on **OK.**

How to Sleep/ Wake Voice Control on Mac

- On the voice control icon on your screen, click on **Sleep** to put the tool to sleep. This means that voice control would not be active at this time.
- Click on **Wake** to bring out the feature from sleep.

How to Select New Language in Voice Control

- Go to the voice control icon and click on the current language at the right side of your screen.

- Select the new language.

How to Choose a Different Microphone for Voice Control

Voice Control is built to use the built-in microphone on your computer by default. You can select another microphone with the steps below

- From the system Dock, click on **System Preferences**

- Tap on **Accessibility**.

- Under the section for Motor, click on **Voice Control** at the left side.

- Navigate to **Microphone** and click on the pull-down menu.

- Select your desired microphone from the list.

How to Disable/ Enable Commands in Voice Control

Here, you would learn how to disable or enable any command available in the voice control feature whether they were created by you or Apple.

- From the system Dock, click on **System Preferences**
- Tap on **Accessibility**.
- Under the section for Motor, click on **Voice Control** at the left side.
- Select the **Command** button at the end of the page.
- Tick the boxes for the commands you want to activate and untick the boxes for the commands to disable.
- Then click on **Done.**

How to Create Custom Commands in Voice Control

Follow the steps below to add personal commands to the voice control feature:

- From the system Dock, click on **System Preferences**

- Tap on **Accessibility**.
- Under the section for Motor, click on **Voice Control** at the left side.
- Select the **Command** button at the end of the page.
- Click on the plus (+) button.
- Go to the box for **When I say** and input your new commands. By default, this command would apply on all apps.
- If you want to use the new command on a specific app, click the pull-down menu beside **While Using**.
- Select the apps to use with the specified custom command.
- Go to the option for **Performed** and select your preferred option from the list.
- Then click on **Done.**

How to Delete Custom Commands in Voice Control

Follow the steps below to permanently delete a custom command in voice controls:

- From the system Dock, click on **System Preferences**
- Tap on **Accessibility**.
- Under the section for Motor, click on **Voice Control** at the left side.
- Select the **Command** button at the end of the page.
- Go to **Custom** and then select the Command you wish to delete.
- Then click on the minus "-"
- And select **Delete** to confirm the action.

How to Receive an Alert for Recognized Commands in Voice Control

Your computer can alert you with a sound any time it recognizes a command.

- From the system Dock, click on **System Preferences**
- Tap on **Accessibility**.
- Under the section for Motor, click on **Voice Control** at the left side.

- Navigate to the bottom of the screen and tick the box beside **Play sound when command is recognized.**

Chapter 10: How to Use Safari on Mac

Safari is the default web browser for the Apple device for surfing the net. The guide below would show you how to use it on your computer. Safari is used to grant you access to any website you wish to view so long as you have the web address.

Steps to Use Picture-in-Picture Feature in Safari

This feature is Apple-Speak that allows you to run a video in its window while running another app. It can be beneficial for multitasking. For instance, you can be watching an important event while also working on the Notes app. This feature has also been added to Safari, you can watch a video in Safari while operating another app. The steps to do this is very simple.

- Go to the page that has the video
- Click and hold the **Volume** icon located in the navigation bar.
- This would display a menu.
- Click on **Enter Picture in Picture** to pull the video into its own window.

- Set to your preferred size and move to the edge of your screen.

How to Visit a Website

- Open the Safari browser from the Finder or the Dock.
- Tap the address bar at the top of the page.
- Input your desired address e.g. www.google.com
- Tap the **Return** key on your keyboard.

How to Bookmark a Website

For faster access to your most loved sites, add the website address to bookmark so that you can just click on it to return to the website at any time.

- Open the Safari browser from the Finder or the Dock.
- Navigate to the web page you want to add to bookmark.
- Press both **Command-D** keys on your keyboard.

- Title your bookmark or leave it with the default title. Input a description if you desire.
- Then tap the **Return** or **Add** key on your keyboard.
- Go to the menu bar located at the left top of your screen.
- Then click on **Show Favorites Bar**.
- You would see the bookmarked ages under the address bar. Click on it to access it. Also, whenever you click on the address bar, you would find your favorite pages listed as suggested sites.

How to Search on the Address Bar

Apart from inputting the website address, you can also input keywords on the address bar to search for your enquiry on Google.

- Open the Safari browser from the Finder or the Dock.
- Tap the address bar at the top of the page.
- Type in your desired query like "release date for the macOS Catalina"

- Tap the **Return** key on your keyboard.
- Safari would then take you to Google where you would see multiple results for your query.

How to Remove Bookmarks

Follow the steps below to remove a bookmarked page from your favorites or bookmarks

- Open the Safari browser from the Finder or the Dock.
- At the top left of your screen, click on **Bookmarks** from the menu bar.
- Then click on **Edit Bookmarks**.
- Tap the arrow beside **Favorites** as that is where the bookmarks are by default.
- Control-click or right-click on the bookmark you want to delete.
- Then select **Delete.**

How to View All Bookmarks

Follow the steps below to view all your bookmarks in one single view

- Open the Safari browser from the Finder or the Dock.
- Beside the address bar, click on the button for **Show sidebar.**
- Tap the bookmarks tab if it is not already showing (this is an open book icon)

How to Add a Web Page to your Reading List

When you add pages to your reading lists, you are able to save the site for reading later. You can also access the reading list even if there is no active internet connection.

- Open the Safari browser from the Finder or the Dock.
- Navigate to the website you wish to add to your reading list.
- Then tap **shift-command-D** keys on your keyboard.
- You would notice a small icon at the sidebar button or the sidebar itself.

How to Enable Private Browsing

When using private browsing, you can surf the internet without the computer saving your search history, sites visited or having the AutoFill information. This is ideal when you do not want anyone to access your browsing data.

- Open the Safari browser from the Finder or the Dock.
- go to the left top of your screen and click on **File** in the menu bar.
- Select **New Private Window** from the drop-down menu.
- Another way is to tap the **shift-command-N** keys on your keyboard.

How to View Your Reading List

- Open the Safari browser from the Finder or the Dock.
- Beside the address bar, tap the **reading list tab**, an icon similar to a pair of glasses.
- Select the item you wish to read to begin reading.

How to Remove items from your Reading Lists

Follow the steps below to remove items you no longer need from your reading list.

- Open the Safari browser from the Finder or the Dock.
- Beside the address bar, tap the **Show sidebar**.
- Click the tab for **reading list,** the icon is similar to a pair of glasses.
- Control click or right-click on the item you want to delete.
- Then select **Remove Item**.

How to Add Extensions to Safari

These are plug-ins that give additional functions to the browser. You can use it to integrate the browser with apps, block ads and other functions. There are several free extensions that you can use to be current with news, increase productivity, provide entertainment, security and lots more. Please note that some of the services or apps that provide these extensions may not be free even if the extension itself is free.

- Open the Safari browser from the Finder or the Dock.
- go to the left top of your screen and click on **Safari** in the menu bar.
- Then click on **Safari Extensions**.
- You would be taken to the App Store's Safari extension page.
- Here you can now download and install extensions in same manner as if you were downloading an app.
- Once the installation is done, launch the app to add it to the toolbar in Safari.

How to Pin Tabs on Safari

This is similar to adding sites to your bookmarks. This feature would pin the tabs to your browser home page so that you can click on it for fast access.

- Open the Safari browser from the Finder or the Dock.
- go to the left top of your screen and click on **View** in the menu bar.

- Then select **Show Tab Bar** from the drop-down.
- Navigate to the website you want to pin down.
- Click and hold down on the website tab and move it to the left side.
- You would see the tab showing the first letter of the site title or as a little site logo at the left side of the tab bar.
- Move the tab to the right to remove it from the pinned tabs list.

How to Set Homepage

When you launch your Homepage, it would take you directly to apple.com. But you can choose a different website to show when you launch your browser.

- Open the Safari browser from the Finder or the Dock.
- go to the left top of your screen and click on **Safari** in the menu bar.
- Go to the tab for **General.**

- Beside option for **Homepage,** input a website.

- Or, you can select **"Set to Current Page"** to use the current page on your browser as your homepage.

- Beside the option for **New windows open with**, tap the **dropdown menu.**

- If you would prefer that a new window opens on your homepage, click on **Homepage.**

- Beside the option for **New tabs open with**, tap the **dropdown menu.**

- If you would prefer that new tabs open on your homepage, click on **Homepage.**

How to Use Reader View

When using reader view, you can pull up web pages in a way that would make it easy to see images and read words without all the programmed movement or animations on the page. Most web pages support this view.

- Go to a website you want to view.

- Click on the button for **Reader View.** this is the lines you see at the left side of the address bar.

How to Share Websites from Safari

Follow the steps below to share a website with family or friends:

- Open the Safari browser from the Finder or the Dock.
- Navigate to the website you want to share.
- You would find the **Share** button at the right top of your screen, click on it.
- Select a method to share the site, either Notes, Emails, AirDrop, Messages, Reminders and any other supported Non-Apple sites.

How to Change Background Color in Reader View

- Go to a website you want to view.
- Click on the button for **Reader View.** this is the lines you see at the left side of the address bar.

- Then tap the **Reader Options** button (this is the AA icon at the right of the address bar)
- Select your preferred background color.

How to Modify Font Size in Reader View

- Go to a website you want to view.
- Click on the button for **Reader View.** this is the lines you see at the left side of the address bar.
- Then tap the **Reader Options** button (this is the AA icon at the right of the address bar).
- Click the smaller "A" icon to reduce text size and the bigger A to increase text size.

How to Modify Font in Reader View

- Go to a website you want to view.
- Click on the button for **Reader View.** this is the lines you see at the left side of the address bar.
- Then tap the **Reader Options** button (this is the AA icon at the right of the address bar)
- Select your preferred font.

How to Customize Favorites in Safari

Follow the steps below to add a website to your list of favorites

- Go to the desired website in Safari.
- Move your pointer on the Smart Search Field.
- Then click on **Favorites.**

If you want to remove a website from your list of favorites, follow the steps below:

- Go to the Safari toolbar and click on **Bookmarks**.
- Then click on **Show Favorites**.
- Use your mouse to right click on the website you want to take out from the list.
- Then click on **Delete**.

How to Organize Your Safari Favorites

- Go to the Safari toolbar and click on **Bookmarks**.
- Then click on **Show Favorites**.
- Move the Favorite to your desired location on the list.

How to Organize Frequently Visited in Safari

With the macOS Catalina, Safari adds websites automatically to your Frequently visited list. Follow the steps below to remove any website from this list

- Go to the Safari toolbar and click on **Bookmarks**.
- Then click on **Show Favorites**.
- Then click on **Show Frequently Visited in Favorites** on the same drop-down.

Follow the steps below to delete a frequently visited site

- Launch your browser, then go to the Favorites page.
- You would see frequently visited sites. Right click on the site you wish to delete.
  - Then click on **Delete.**

How to Access Siri Suggestions

- Go to the Safari toolbar and click on **Bookmarks**.
- Then click on **Show Favorites**.
- Navigate to Siri Suggestions on the next screen and click on any desired web page.

Chapter 11: Conclusion

With all the teachings in this book, I am confident that you would be able to fully enjoy all the amazing features of the macOS Catalina on your Mac.

I have ensured that everything you need to know regarding the macOS Catalina is covered in this book to help you maximize your experience on your Mac

If you are pleased with the content of this book, don't forget to recommend this book to a friend.

Thank you.

Other Books by The Same Author

- THE iPhone XS AND XS MAX USER GUIDE

  https://amzn.to/2kgrHJ2

- The iPhone XR User Guide

  https://amzn.to/2miQay8

- THE IPHONE X USER GUIDE

  https://amzn.to/2lQE6Uw

- Samsung Galaxy Note 10 User Guide

  https://amzn.to/2MbH3d9

- iPhone 11 User Guide

  https://amzn.to/32bObMa

- iPhone 11 Pro User Guide

  https://amzn.to/2nGAvtz

- iPhone 11 Pro Max User Guide

  https://amzn.to/2MBLixt

- Mastering the iOS 13

  https://amzn.to/2MHlr7A

Printed in Great
Britain
by Amazon

31297135R00080